Crazy Creature Number Puzzles

STUDIO D

Sterling Publishing Co., Inc. **New York**

By the Same Authors
Crazy Creature Picture Puzzles
Picture Puzzles for the Super-Smart

The answer to the puzzle on
the title page is 10.

Copyright © 1986 by Irit Adler and Shem Levy
Published by Sterling Publishing Co., Inc.
Two Park Avenue, New York, N.Y. 10016
Distributed in Canada by Oak Tree Press Ltd.
% Canadian Manda Group, P.O. Box 920, Station U
Toronto, Ontario, Canada M8Z 5P9
Distributed in Australia by Capricorn Ltd.
P.O. Box 665, Lane Cove, NSW 2066
Manufactured in the United States of America
All rights reserved

Library of Congress Cataloging-in-Publication Data

Crazy creature number puzzles.

Includes index.
Summary: A collection of mathematical puzzles designed
to encourage intuitive and logical thinking.
1. Mathematical recreations—Juvenile literature.
[1. Mathematical recreations] I. Studio D.
QA95.C73 1986   793.7'4   86-5981
ISBN 0-8069-4750-0
ISBN 0-8069-4752-7 (pbk.)
ISBN 0-8069-4751-9 (lib. bdg.)

Contents

Introduction

This book offers young readers a different perspective on math. The puzzles in it aren't the ordinary math being taught (and practised) at school, though they are derived from the same basic logic. While ordinary math teaches children coherent organized logical thinking, these puzzles work on another aspect of the thinking process—that of intuition and insight. A bright mind should blend both aspects.

The puzzles in this book are designed to defy ordinary school-like solutions and will therefore encourage and inspire children to think in an original way. They will also improve the child's mathematical and logical perceptions with the addition of an intuitive non-algorithmic ingredient which is unfortunately lacking in the ordinary study of math.

At first glance, some of the puzzles may seem difficult. But they all involve only elementary arithmetic that won't present any problem to children who can add, subtract, multiply and divide. They look different from the puzzles we're used to seeing in textbooks. But they aren't more difficult and are much more fun to look at!

The famous Fibonacci series can serve as an example of the intuitive process I am referring to. The series is: 1,1,2,3,5,8,13. What is the next number in the series? Even adults who haven't done much math often have trouble finding it.

Don't start looking for powers and roots. Each number in this series is simply the sum of the two previous numbers. Children of six can, in principle, solve that. But will they? This is where insights come in.

This series can also serve as an example of the beauty of Number Theory. If you calculate the differences between each two adjacent numbers in the series, you get: 0,1,1,2,3,5,. . . Now note what has happened: The rule of the series still applies! Now find the series of differences of that new series: 1,0,1,1,2,. . . And bingo—the magic works again! You can keep doing that ad infinitum and it will always work. Why wasn't I taught such magic when I was six or seven? It might have altered my entire aversion to math, which I finally got rid of only at the university level.

The final chapter of this book introduces a completely innovative approach to teaching math. The idea behind it is that the study of elementary logic should precede that of math. The puzzles in that chapter introduce the idea of formal systems. The basic logic of formal systems is the same as that of math, both having axioms and rules of operation. Number Theory and geometry can thus be viewed as specific cases of formal systems.

Once you get children thinking in terms of axioms and rules of operation, which can be done through puzzle-solving, you've got them thinking in terms of the basic logic of Math, whether they realize it or not. Then it becomes a simple matter to introduce mathematical concepts with their axioms and rules. Not only are the children ready and eager for them, but they're also giant steps ahead.

I am deeply indebted to Douglas R. Hofstadter. It was while reading his greatly illuminating book, *Godel, Escher, Bach: An Eternal Golden Braid* (Penguin Books, 1980), that I developed the ideas presented in the last chapter of this book.

What Next?

The creatures in this book may be crazy-looking, but the numbers in their bodies are always *logical*.

For example, let's take the series

$$1-2-3-4-5-?$$

You can see right away that all you're doing is adding 1 to each number. So the question mark, obviously, stands for 6.

When you find out what the logic of a series is, you'll always be able to tell what number comes next.

What number should replace the question mark in these puzzles?

1. Creepy

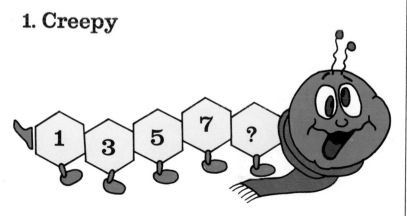

Answer on page 90.

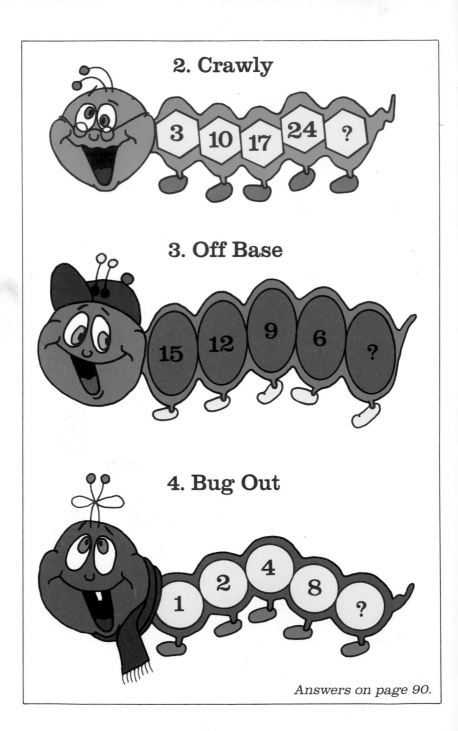

2. Crawly

3 10 17 24 ?

3. Off Base

15 12 9 6 ?

4. Bug Out

1 2 4 8 ?

Answers on page 90.

5. Totem Pole

6. Coots and Ladders

Answers on page 90.

Now the puzzles get a little trickier. This time, you'll be dealing with a pair of numbers—not just one. What comes next?

7. Double Creepy

8. Double Crawly

Answers on page 90.

9. Come Fly with Me

10. Heavy!

Answers on page 90.

11

Since you did so well thinking about two numbers, want to try for three?

What numbers should replace the question marks in these stumpers?

11. MOO-ving Right Along

12. MOO-re Numbers

Answers on page 90.

13. You're Getting Me Down

14. Pinball

Answers on page 90.

13

In the next puzzles, the question mark is not the NEXT item in the series—but the last one!

15. Speedy

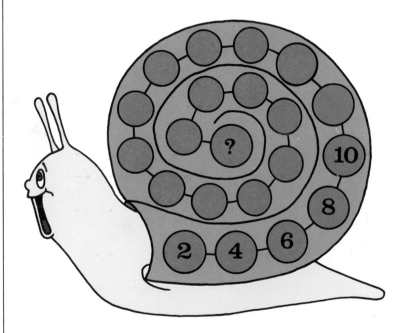

Answer on page 90.

16. Sea Serpent

Answer on page 90.

17. Dino the Dinosaur

Answer on page 90.

What's the Big Idea?

There is some idea—some logic—to the number set-ups in each creature's stomach.

What numbers should replace the question marks?

18. Hi, There!

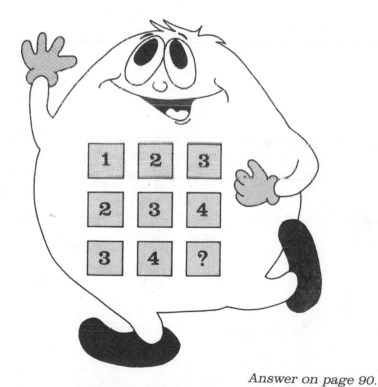

Answer on page 90.

19. Something Fishy

Answer on page 90.

20. The Nervy Nine

Answer on page 90.

21. Nine for Dinner

Answer on page 90.

22. Building Blocks

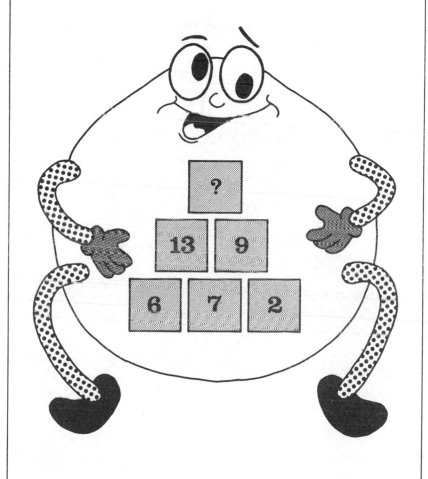

Answer on page 91.

23. Pizza Pete

Answer on page 91.

24. The Athletes

Answer on page 91.

25. The Cheerleaders

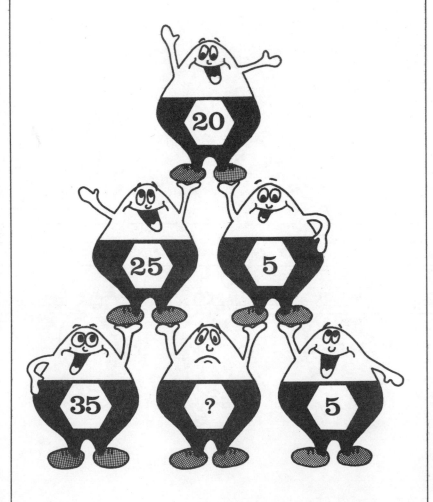

Answer on page 91.

A little bit different? Not really!

26. Seal Circus

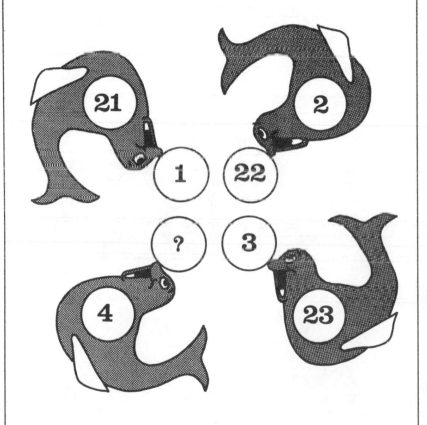

Answer on page 91.

27. Ate Too Much

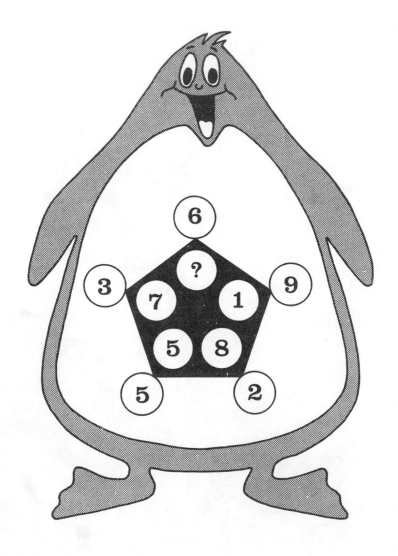

Answer on page 91.

28. Water Ballet

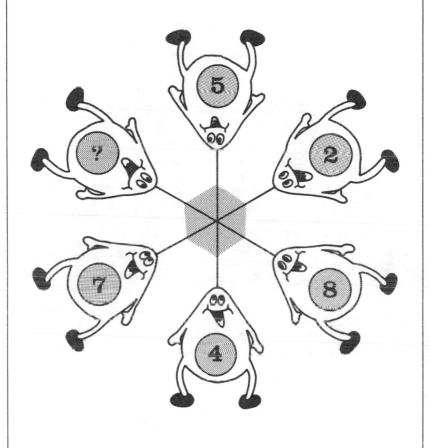

Answer on page 91.

29. Peacock Power

Answer on page 91.

Nutty Notes

One of these notes is not like the others . . .
Which one?

30. Singing in the Rain

Answer on page 91.

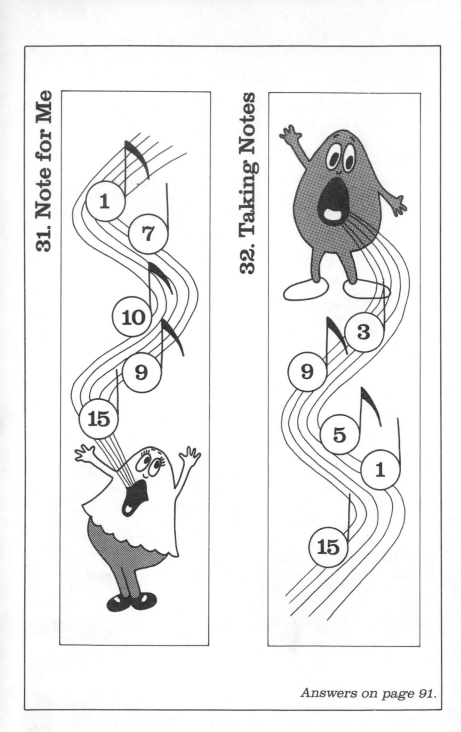

Answers on page 91.

33. They're Playing Our Song

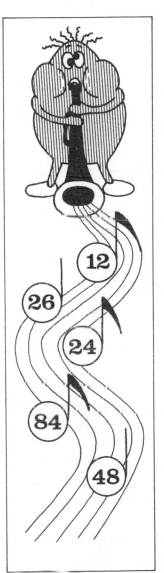

34. Come Blow Your Horn

Answers on page 91.

35. And Then We Wrote . . .

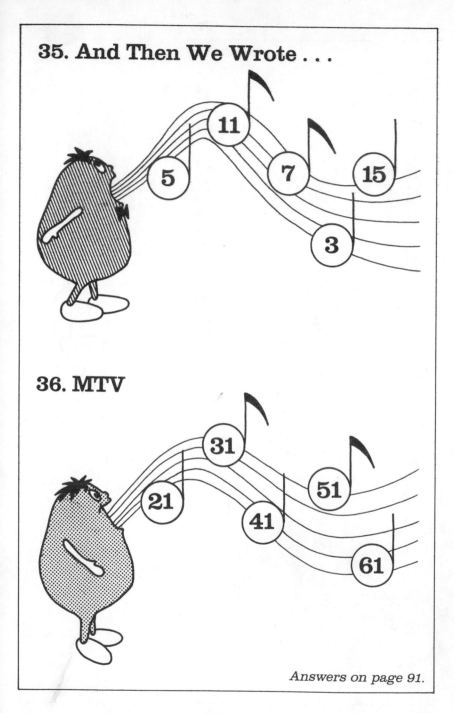

36. MTV

Answers on page 91.

I've Got Your Number!

Can you get the number in the Daddy creature by
- + (adding)
- − (subtracting)
- ÷ (dividing)
- × (multiplying)

the numbers in the Baby creature?

You can use a Baby's number only once!

37. Killer Bees

Answer on page 91.

Hint: You don't have to use the Baby numbers in the same order that they appear in the picture.

38. Glee Club

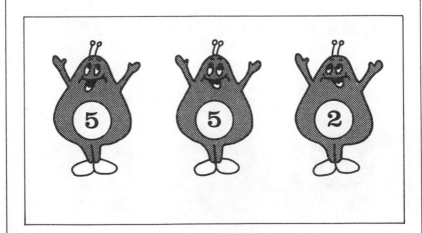

Answer on page 91.

39. Saved by the Bell

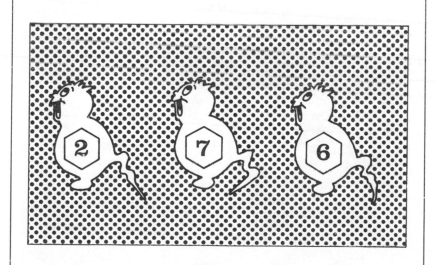

Answer on page 91.

40. Aerobics

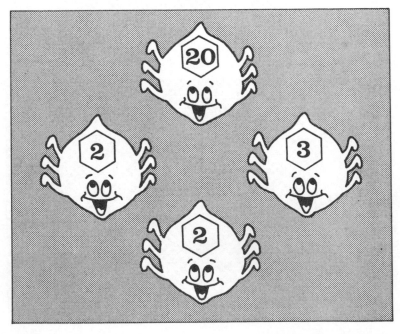

Answer on page 91.

The next puzzles are a bit different—but not much. Every creature has swallowed a simple math idea. The picture tells you everything you need to know—except WHAT easy arithmetic operation you need to use to make the idea work.

Instead of a question mark—or a black space—you get a symbol. In "Nessie" the symbol is a triangle.

What does it stand for— +
—
×
or ÷ ?

41. Nessie

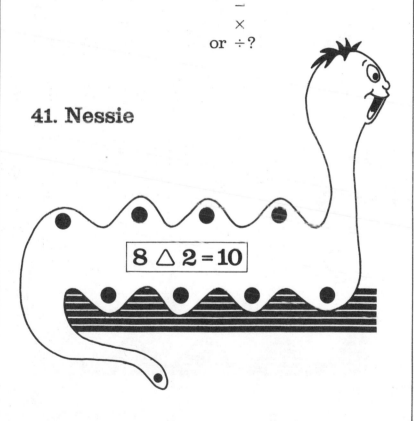

$$8 \triangle 2 = 10$$

Answer on page 91.

Here you're looking for more than one arithmetic operation. What do the symbols stand for in these wacky worms?

42. Wiggly

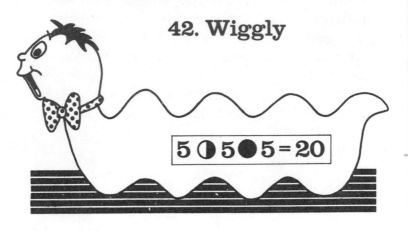

$$5 \circ 5 \bullet 5 = 20$$

43. Wriggley

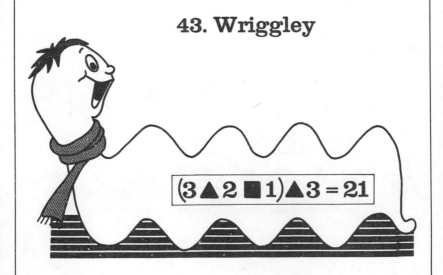

$$(3 \blacktriangle 2 \blacksquare 1) \blacktriangle 3 = 21$$

Answers on page 92.

Bunch of Squares

The first squares in this chapter are called Magic Squares. What makes them magical? Add the numbers in a magic square in any direction—and you always get the same answer!

In these magic squares, we give you the answer and all the numbers you need to fill up the spaces. We even put some of them in for you. Can you do the rest?

Get out your pencil, a good eraser and plenty of scratch paper for these cuties!

48.
The Mad
Magician

Arrange numbers 1—9 so that the magic total in every direction is 15.

Answer on page 92.

49. Omar the Ostrich

18		
	12	
	20	

Arrange the numbers 4, 6, 8, 10, 12, 14, 16, 18 and 20 so that the magic sum is 36.

Answer on page 92.

50. Roller Derby

Arrange the numbers 1–16 so that the magic sum is 34.

Answer on page 92.

51. The Tricky Twin

This is just like the last puzzle, Roller Derby. Use the same numbers (1–16) and come up with the same magic sum (34). *But do it in a different way!*

Answer on page 92.

More squares! But they're not magical this time. All you have to do is count them. Easy? Ha! Don't be fooled!

How many squares are there in each creature?

52. Skateboard Sam

Answer on page 92.

53. Scooter Squares

Answer on page 92.

54. The Wild One

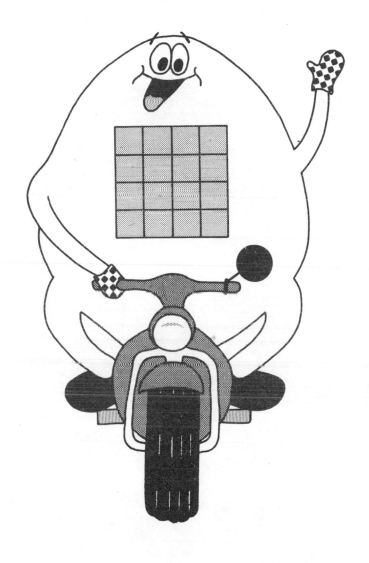

Answer on page 92.

55. Going Nowhere

Answer on page 92.

Nifty Numbers

In every one of the puzzles in this chapter you'll find more number setups—just like the ones you did earlier. Each creature has a logic of its own. What number should replace the question mark?

56. Escaped Convict

Answer on page 90.

57. Fins

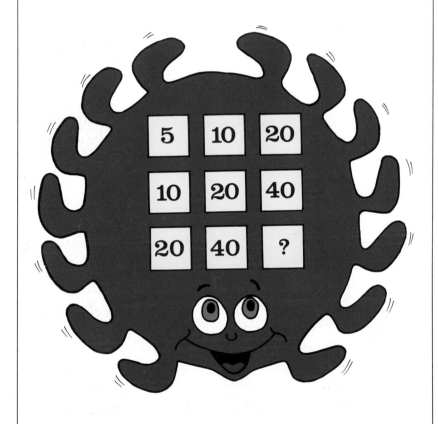

Answer on page 92.

58. Party Hats

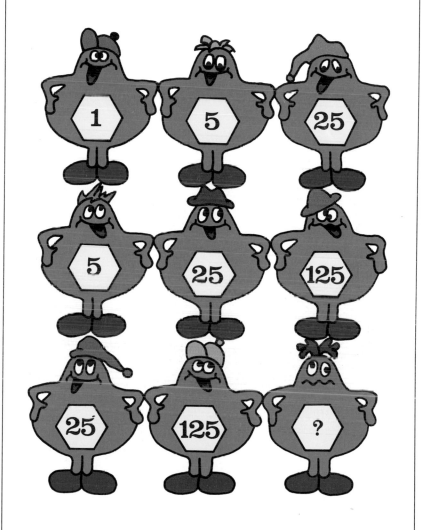

Answer on page 92.

59. The Winning Team

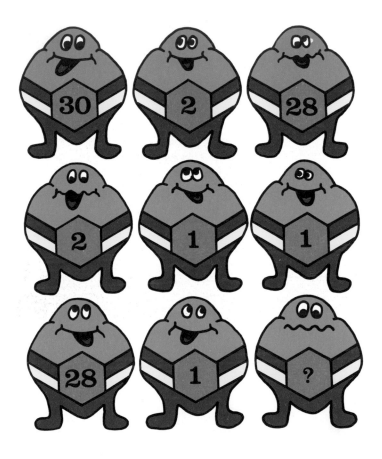

Answer on page 92.

60. Puzzlement

Answer on page 92.

61. Sitting Pretty

Answer on page 93.

62. Pyramid People

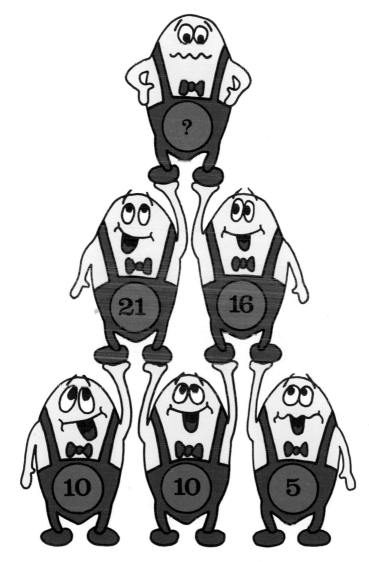

Answer on page 93.

63. True Blue

Answer on page 93.

64. Going Buggy

Answer on page 93.

65. The Twilight Zone

Answer on page 93.

66. Donna the Dragonfly

Answer on page 93.

67. Quasar Quartet

Answer on page 93.

Party Games

All the creatures in this chapter are playing party games. And while they're playing, they're giving you more number progressions (a lot like the ones in the first chapter—but crazier!).

What number should replace the question mark in these puzzles?

68. Telephone

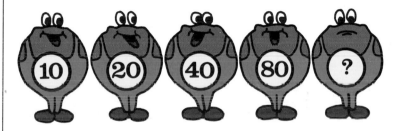

69. Tug o' War

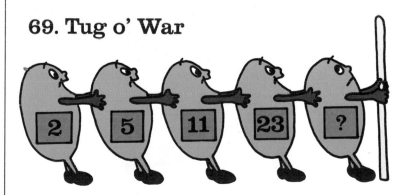

Answers on page 93.

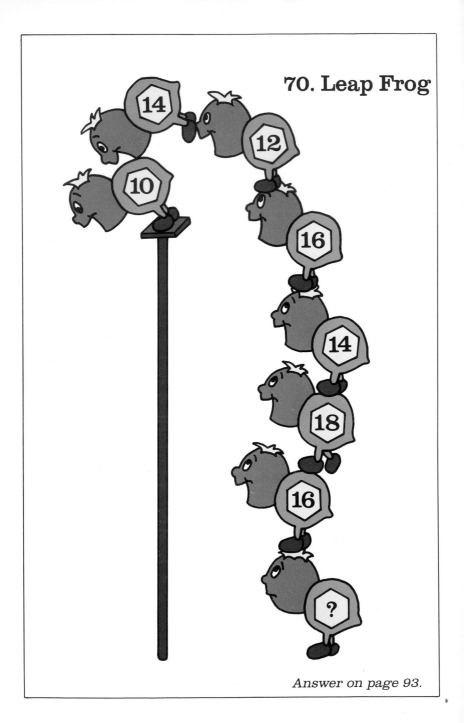

70. Leap Frog

Answer on page 93.

71. Rattlesnake

Answer on page 93.

72. Team Relay

Answer on page 93.

73. Musical Chairs

74. Charades

Answers on page 93.

1 1

2 2

3 4

8 4

? ?

7 6

12 10

4 1

8 4

10 ?

Answers on page 93 and 94.

77. Monkey See Monkey Do

Answer on page 94.

78. Balloon Baseball

79. Follow the Leader

Answers on page 94.

Marvelous Misfits

One of the couples in each of the next puzzles is not like the others. Can you find the misfits?

80. Square Dance

Bruno and Bertha

Clem and Chloe

Roscoe and Rowena

Harold and Helga

Amos and Anita

Answer on page 94.

81. Balancing Acts

Leo
and Lolita

Mick and Bianca

Tom and Tina

Elvis
and Edwina

Garfield and Garbo

Answer on page 94.

82. Back to Back

Jack and Jill

Dancer and Prancer

Hansel and Gretel

Moe and Flo

Lester and Hester

Answer on page 94.

83. The Last Dance

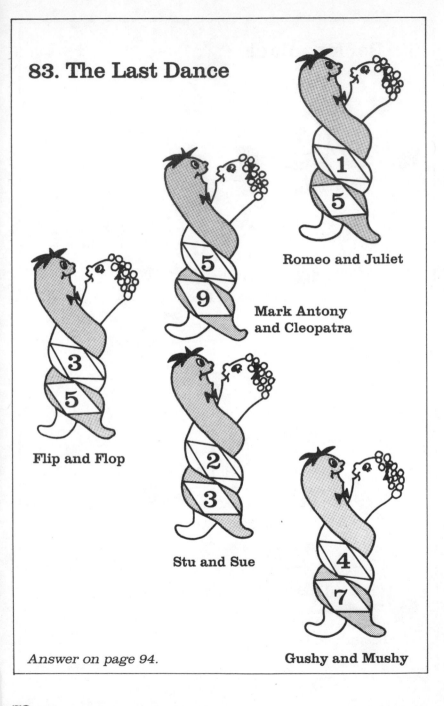

Romeo and Juliet

Mark Antony
and Cleopatra

Flip and Flop

Stu and Sue

Gushy and Mushy

Answer on page 94.

Bringing Up Baby

Can you get to the number in the Baby Creature by using each number in the Daddy or Mommy creature just once? The only help you get (same as in Chapter 4) is that you can use simple arithmetic operations to do the job:

+ (adding)
− (subtracting)
× (multiplying)
÷ (or dividing)
in any combination.

84. Flying Lesson

Answer on page 94.

85. Telling Snail Jokes

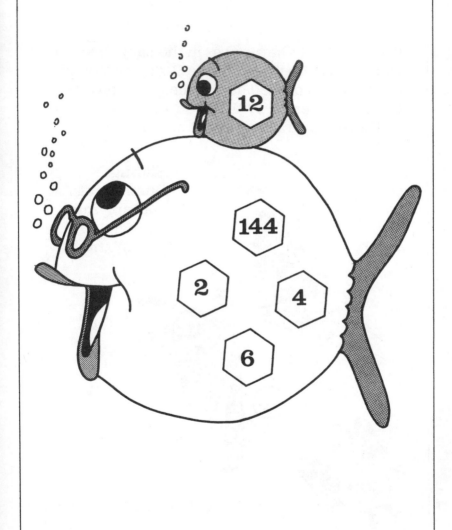

Answer on page 94.

86. Telling Fish Jokes

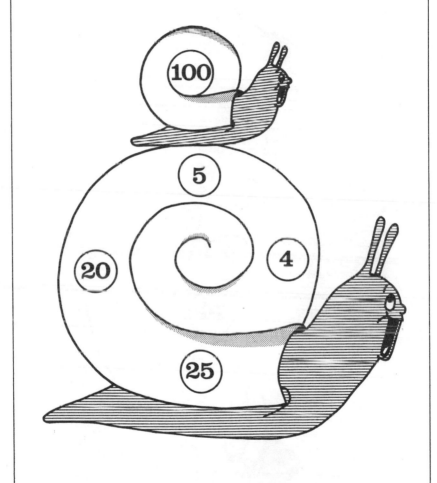

Answer on page 94.

87. Up from Down Under

Answer on page 94.

Multi-Magic Squares

As on pages 41 to 44, the puzzles in this chapter are Magic Squares. They're magic, you'll remember, because they add up to the same "magic" number in any direction: up, down or across!

**88.
Square
in the
Round**

Can you arrange the numbers 14–22 so that the magic sum is 54?

Answer on page 94.

89. You Don't Look 135!

Arrange the numbers 5, 15, 25, 35, 45, 55, 65, 75 and 85 so that the magic sum is 135.

Answer on page 94.

90. Fifty-Fifty

Arrange the numbers 5–20 so that the magic sum is 50.

Answer on page 95.

91. Too Many Square Meals

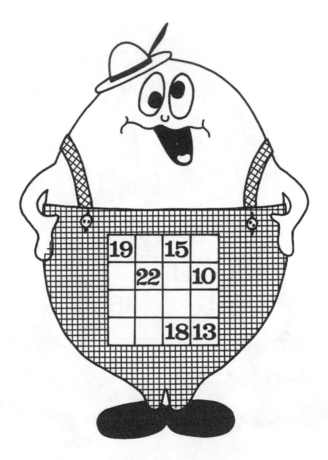

Arrange the numbers 10–25 so that the magic sum is 70.

Answer on page 95.

Word
Production

And now for something really different. In this new kind of puzzle, you get a letter (or a little string of letters) and a few rules about what you can and can't do with them. You can apply the rules in any order and as many times as you want. The goal? To produce the word that is the title of the puzzle!

Turn the page to get to the first puzzle.

92. FLY

Can you produce **FLY**?

Start with: the letter F

Rule I: You may add Y's to the right of F in bunches of 3.

Rule II: You may replace any string of 5 Y's with an L.

How to work Rule I:

Example: 1. F
2. FYYY (correct) *or*
   1. F
   2. FYYYYYY (correct)
but not
1. F
2. FYYYY (wrong. You can only add the Y's in bunches of 3s.)

How to work Rule II:

Example: 1. F
2. FYYYYYYYYY (by applying Rule I)
3. FYYYYL (by Rule II)
   or
1. F
2. FYYYYYYYYYY
3. FYYLYY

Can you now produce **FLY**?

Answer on page 95.

93. SUPER

Can you produce **SUPER**?

Start with: the string SU.

Rule I: You may add any even number of Rs to the right of SU.

Rule II: You may replace any string of 4 Rs with a string of 2 Es (Note: only 4 for 2—not 2 for 1!).

Rule III: You may replace any string of RE with a P.

How to work Rule I:

Example: 1. SU
2. SURR (correct)
   or
1. SU
2. SURRRRR (correct)
   but not
1. SU
2. SURRR (incorrect, because 3 is an odd number)

How to work Rule II:

Example: 1. SU
2. SURRRR (applying Rule I)
3. SUEE (by Rule II)
   or
1. SU
2. SURRRRRR (by Rule I)
3. SUREER (by Rule II)

How to work Rule III:

Example: 1. SU
2. SURRRRRR (by Rule I)
3. SURREE (by Rule II)
4. SURPE (by Rule III)

Can you now produce **SUPER**?

Answer on page 95.

94. SMART

Can you produce **SMART**?

Start with: the string SM.

Rule I: You may add any odd number of Ts to the right of SM.

Rule II: You may replace any string of 2 Ts with an A.

Rule III: You may replace any string of ATT with an R.

How to work Rule I:

Example: 1. SM
       2. SMTTT (correct)
          but not
       1. SM
       3. SMTTTT (incorrect because 4 is an even number)

How to work Rule II:

Example: 1. SM
       2. SMTTT (applying Rule I)
       3. SMTA (by Rule II)

How to work Rule III:

       1. SM
       2. SMTTTTT (by Rule I)
       3. SMATTT (by Rule II)
       4. SMRT (by Rule III)

Can you now produce **SMART**?

Answer on page 95.

95. LOGIC

Can you produce **LOGIC**?

Start with: G

Rule I: You may add ICs to the right of G in groups of 4.

Rule II: You may replace 2 ICs with a G.

Rule III: If you get the sequence GIC, you can cross it out.

Rule IV: You may replace a GG with a LO.

How to work Rule I:

Example: 1. G
2. GICICICIC

How to work Rule II:

Example: 1. G
2. GICICICIC (applying Rule I)
3. GICICG (by Rule II)

How to work Rule III:

Example: 1. G
2. GICICICIC (by Rule I)
3. ICICIC (by Rule III)

How to work Rule IV:

Example: 1. G
2. GICICICIC (by Rule I)
3. GGICIC (by Rule II)
4. LOICIC (by Rule IV)

Can you now produce **LOGIC**?

Answer on page 95.

Answers

1. **Creepy:** 9. The numbers increase by 2.
2. **Crawly:** 31. The numbers increase by 7.
3. **Off Base:** 3. The numbers decrease by 3.
4. **Bug Out:** 16. The numbers double.
5. **Totem Pole:** 81. The numbers multiply by 3.
6. **Coots and Ladders:** 3. The sequence is +9, −8, +9. So another −8 will get us to 3 (11−8=3).
7. **Double Creepy** (top): 2
   (bottom): 2
   Each number decreases by 2.
8. **Double Crawly** (top): 5. Numbers increase by 1.
   (bottom): 1. Numbers decrease by 1.
9. **Come Fly With Me:** 18. The numbers on the right are always one less than the numbers on the left.
10. **Heavy!:** 2. When you add together the numbers on the left and those on the right, the total always increases by 1.
11. **Moo-ving Right Along:** 4. The sum of each column, when added vertically, is 12.
12. **Moo-re Numbers:** 9. The bottom number is always the sum of the top two numbers.
13. **You're Getting Me Down:** 10. The middle number is the sum of the numbers on the right and left.
14. **Pinball:** 25. The number on the left is the sum of the other two numbers, divided by two.
15. **Speedy:** 42. The numbers increase by 2.
16. **Sea Serpent:** 5. The numbers decrease by 5.
17. **Dino the Dinosaur:** 92. The *differences* between the numbers increase by 1.
18. **Hi, There!:** 5. The numbers in each row and column increase by 1.
19. **Something Fishy:** 10. The numbers in each row and column increase by 2.
20. **The Nervy Nine:** 70. The numbers on the right are the sum of those in the left and middle columns.
21. **Nine for Dinner:** 5. Each number is half the one to the left.

22. Building Blocks: 22. Each block shows the sum of the two blocks below it ($6 + 7 = 13$, $7 + 2 = 9$ and, therefore, $13 + 9 = 22$).

23. Pizza Pete: 10. Each pizza shows the sum of the two pizzas below it ($10 + 5 = 15$, $5 + 5 = 10$, and, therefore, $15 + 10 = 25$).

24. The Athletes: 7. Each number on the athletes' sweaters is the *difference* between the numbers on the left and right sweaters below ($10 - 2 = 8$, $25 - 10 = 15$ and, therefore, $15 - 8 = 7$).

25. The Cheerleaders: 10. Each number is the difference between the number on the lower left and the number above ($25 - 20 = 5$, $35 - 25 = 10$ and therefore, $10 - 5 = 5$).

26. Seal Circus: 24. Two series are at work here. They both start from the upper left and take turns moving in and out of the seals.

27. Ate Too Much: 4. Each pair of numbers (the one in the corner and the one nearest it on the outside of the creature's inner stomach) adds up to 10.

28. Water Ballet: 1. The opposite numbers are pairs that add up to 9.

29. Peacock Power: 3. This peacock has matching feathers: the bottom ones on either side add up to 5 ($4 + 1$ and $2 + 3$); the ones in the middle add up to 6 ($1 + 5$ and $3 + 3$); and the ones nearest the head add up to 7 ($6 + 1$ and therefore $4 + 3$).

30. Singing in the Rain: 45. It is the only odd number.

31. Note for Me: 10. It's the only even number.

32. Taking Notes: 15. It's the only 2-digit number.

33. They're Playing Our Song: 6. It's the only one-digit number.

34. Come Blow Your Horn: 26. It's the only number that can't be divided by 3 and 4.

35. "And Then We Wrote . . .": 15. It is the only number here that is not a prime number (divisible by no other number besides 1 and itself).

36. MTV: 21. It is the only one that is not a prime number (see above).

37. Killer Bees: $5 \times 6 = 30$. $30 + 1 = 31$.

38. Glee Club: $2 \times 5 = 10$. $10 + 5 = 15$. *or* $5 - 2 = 3$. $3 \times 5 = 15$.

39. Saved by the Bell: $2 \times 7 = 14$. $14 + 6 = 20$.

40. Aerobics: $20 + 2 = 22$. $22 + 3 = 25$. $25 \times 2 = 50$.

41. Nessie: $\triangle = +$. $8 + 2 = 10$.

42. **Wiggly:** $\mathbb{O} = \times$ and $\bullet = -$. $5 \times 5 = 25$. $25 - 5 = 20$.

43. **Wriggley:** $\blacktriangle = \times$ and $\blacksquare = +$. $3 \times 2 = 6$. $6 + 1 = 7$. $7 \times 3 = 21$.

44. **Walter:** $\bigcirc = +$ and $\bullet = \times$. $1 + 2 = 3$. $3 + 3 = 6$. $6 \times 4 = 24$.

45. **Wanda:** $\blacktriangledown = \times$ and $\triangledown = -$. $10 \times 10 = 100$. $100 - 8 = 92$. $4 \times 2 = 8$.

46. **Worm at Rest:** $\lozenge = \times$ and $\bigcirc = -$. $10 \times 10 = 100$. $100 - 10 = 90$.

47. **Bookworm:** $\blacksquare = \div$ and $\blacksquare = +$. $90 \div 2 = 45$. $45 \div 3 = 15$. $15 + 5 = 20$.

48. **The Mad Magician:**

2	9	4
7	5	3
6	1	8

49. **Omar the Ostrich:**

18	4	14
8	12	16
10	20	6

50. **Roller Derby:**

6	3	9	16
12	13	7	2
15	10	4	5
1	8	14	11

51. **The Tricky Twin:**

11	2	5	16
7	14	9	4
10	3	8	13
6	15	12	1

52. **Skateboard Sam:** 5.

53. **Scooter Squares:** 14.

54. **The Wild One:** 30.

55. **Going Nowhere:** 55.

56. **Escaped Convict:** 250. Not only does each row multiply horizontally, but the columns also multiply vertically. ($5 \times 5 = 25$. $5 \times 2 = 10$. $25 \times 10 = 250$.)

57. **Fins:** 80. Each number is multiplied by 2. ($5 \times 2 = 10$; $10 \times 2 = 20$. $10 \times 2 = 20$; $20 \times 2 = 40$. $20 \times 2 = 40$; $40 \times 2 = 80$.)

58. **Party Hats:** 625. Each number is multiplied by 5. ($1 \times 5 = 5$; $5 \times 5 = 25$. $25 \times 5 = 125$. $125 \times 5 = 625$.)

59. **The Winning Team:** 27. The numbers in the middle column are the difference between the left-hand and right-hand column numbers. ($30 - 2 = 28$. $2 - 1 = 1$. $28 - 1 = 27$.)

60. **Puzzlement:** 54. Each number is the product of the two numbers under it. ($2 \times 3 = 6$. $3 \times 3 = 9$. $6 \times 9 = 54$.)

92

61. **Sitting Pretty:** 2. The same process, but this time, divide. ($25 \div 5 = 5$. $250 \div 25 = 10$. $10 \div 5 = 2$.)

62. **Pyramid People:** 38. Each number is the result of adding the two numbers beneath it—plus 1. ($10 + 10 = 20$. $20 + 1 = 21$. $10 + 5 = 15$. $15 + 1 = 16$. $21 + 16 = 37$. $37 + 1 = 38$.)

63. **True Blue:** 10. Each number is the average of the two numbers beneath it (the numbers beneath it added and then divided by 2). ($10 + 6 = 16$; $16 \div 2 = 8$. $6 + 18 = 24$; $24 \div 2 = 12$. $8 + 12 = 20$; $20 \div 2 = 10$.)

64. **Going Buggy:** 9. Each pair of numbers, multiplied together, comes to 72.

65. **The Twilight Zone:** 8. The outer number is always 5 more than the inner number.

66. **Donna the Dragonfly:** 2. Multiply the numbers in each set of wings and the product is identical. (Back wings: $5 \times 2 = 10$; $10 \times 1 = 10$. Middle wings: $3 \times 4 = 12$; $2 \times 6 = 12$; Front wings: $8 \times 1 = 8$, and therefore, $4 \times 2 = 8$.)

67. **Quasar Quartet:** 3. Same as #66. ($2 \times 3 = 6$; $6 \times 1 = 6$. $12 \times 1 = 12$; $6 \times 2 = 12$. $9 \times 2 = 18$; $6 \times 3 = 18$.)

68. **Telephone:** 160. Each number is multiplied by 2.

69. **Tug o' War:** 47. Each number is multiplied by 2 and then has 1 added to it ($2 \times 2 = 4$. $4 + 1 = 5$. $5 \times 2 = 10$. $10 + 1 = 11$. $11 \times 2 = 22$. $22 + 1 = 23$. $23 \times 2 = 46$. $46 + 1 = 47$.)

70. **Leap Frog:** 20. The numbers advance $+4$ and then $-$(minus) 2.

71. **Rattlesnake:** 16. The differences between the numbers increase by 1. ($2 - 1 = 1$; $4 - 2 = 2$; $7 - 4 = 3$; $11 - 7 = 4$ and therefore $16 - 11 = 5$.)

72. **Team Relay:** 21. This is the famous Fibonacci series. With the exception of the first two numbers (1 and 1), each number is the sum of the two numbers that come before it.

73. **Musical Chairs:** top: 6 bottom: 16. The upper row advances by adding 1 to each number. The bottom row advances by multiplying each number by 2.

74. **Charades:** 1. Add the pair of numbers in each creature ($1 + 1 = 2$; $3 + 1 = 4$; $6 + 2 = 8$; $14 + 2 = 16$) and you see that the sums of the numbers multiplies by 2 each time. Therefore, the last pair must add up to 32, and the answer must be 1.

75. **Shoe Scramble** (Left): 5. (Right): 16. Two series are at work. One starts at the left of the top creature and zigzags to the right of the second creature, then to the left of the next

creature: 1-2-3-4-5. The other series starts at the top right and zigzags down, multiplying by 2: 1-2-4-8-16.

76. Balloon Basketball: 5. The *differences* between the left and right boxes of each creature increase by 1: $7 - 6 = 1$; $12 - 10 = 2$; $4 - 1 = 3$; $8 - 4 = 4$—a series of 1-2-3-4. Therefore $10 - 5 = 5$, to complete the series.

77. Monkey See Monkey Do: Top: 3. Middle: 2. Bottom: 2. Higher numbers enter from the top.

78. Balloon Baseball: 8. Add the numbers in each creature ($14 + 14 + 2 = 30$. $10 + 5 + 10 = 25$. $6 + 7 + 7 = 20$. $5 + 5 + 5 = 15$.) You see that each sum reduces by 5. Therefore, the last sum has to add up to 10 and the missing number is 8.

79. Follow the Leader: 7, 2 and 1, in any order. Multiply the numbers in each creature: $1 \times 2 = 2 \times 3 = 6$. $2 \times 2 = 4 \times 2 = 8$. $2 \times 5 = 10 \times 1 = 10$. $3 \times 2 = 6 \times 2 = 12$. Therefore the last trio should add up to 14, and the only whole numbers you can multiply together to get 14 are 7, 2 and 1.

80. Square Dance: Roscoe and Rowena. The boy's number is always 3 times the girl's number, except for Roscoe's.

81. Balancing Acts: Mick and Bianca. The number of the bottom creature is always the top creature's number squared—except for Bianca. (Squared means the number is multiplied by itself.)

82. Back to Back: Lester and Hester. Every couple's numbers add up to 25, except Lester and Hester.

83. The Last Dance: Romeo and Juliet. The lower number of each couple is always twice the upper number—minus 1! Except for Romeo and Juliet.

84. Flying Lesson: $5 \times 4 = 20$. $20 \times 15 = 300$. $300 \div 3 = 100$.

85. Telling Snail Jokes: $6 + 2 + 4 = 12$. $144 \div 12 = 12$.

86. Telling Fish Jokes: $20 \times 4 = 80$. $80 + 25 = 105$. $105 - 5 = 100$.

87. Up from Down Under: $11 + 14 = 25$. $75 \div 3 = 25$. $25 \times 25 = 625$.

88. Square in the Round:

17	16	21
22	18	14
15	20	19

89. You Don't Look 135!:

15	85	35
65	45	25
55	5	75

90. Fifty-Fifty:

12	14	19	5
15	9	8	18
6	20	13	11
17	7	10	16

91. Too Many Square Meals:

19	12	15	24
17	22	21	10
20	11	16	23
14	25	18	13

92. FLY: 1. F. 2. FYYYYYY (by rule I). 3. FLY (by rule II).

93. SUPER: 1. SU. 2. SURRRRRR (by rule I). 3. SUREER (by rule II). 4. SUPER (by rule III).

94. SMART: 1. SM. 2. SMTTTTTTT (by rule I). 3. SMAATTT (by rule II). 4. SMART (by rule III).

95. LOGIC: 1. G. 2. GICICICICICICIC (by rule I). 3. GGGG-ICIC (by rule II). 4. GGGIC (by rule III). 5. LOGIC (by rule IV).

ABOUT THE AUTHORS

Shem Levy studied political science and psychology at Tel Aviv University before doing graduate work at the University of Chicago. On his return to Israel, he founded High Q, a school that prepares people to take standardized university entrance tests. His students were not only enthusiastic about the puzzles he devised—and had great fun solving them—but they also did wonders on the tests.

Also a native of Tel Aviv, Irit Adler taught several courses in the graphic arts after graduating with honors from art school. She later joined one of Israel's most prominent advertising agencies and was soon promoted to the post of chief art director.

In 1984 Irit and Shem joined forces to establish Studio D, and this book is their fourth collaboration.

Index